3 4028 09008 1697
HARRIS COUNTY PUBLIC LIBRARY

J 629.222 Cru
Cruz, Calvin
Porsche 918 Spyder

WITHDRAWN

$24.95
ocn907158239

D0880862

PORSCHE
918 SPYDER

BY CALVIN CRUZ

BELLWETHER MEDIA • MINNEAPOLIS, MN

Are you ready to take it to the extreme?
Torque books thrust you into the action-packed world
of sports, vehicles, mystery, and adventure. These books
may include dirt, smoke, fire, and dangerous stunts.
WARNING: read at your own risk.

This edition first published in 2016 by Bellwether Media, Inc.

No part of this publication may be reproduced in whole or in part without written permission of the publisher.
For information regarding permission, write to Bellwether Media, Inc., Attention: Permissions Department,
5357 Penn Avenue South, Minneapolis, MN 55419.

Library of Congress Cataloging-in-Publication Data

Cruz, Calvin, author.
  Porsche 918 Spyder / by Calvin Cruz.
    pages cm -- (Torque: Car crazy)
  Summary: "Engaging images accompany information about Porsche 918 Spyder. The combination
of high-interest subject matter and light text is intended for students in grades 3 through 7"--Provided by
publisher.
  Includes bibliographical references and index.
  Audience: Ages 7-12.
  Audience: Grades 3-7.
  ISBN 978-1-62617-285-2 (hardcover : alk. paper)
  1. Porsche automobiles--Juvenile literature. I. Title.
TL215.P75C75 2016
629.222'2--dc23
                                        2015011133

Text copyright © 2016 by Bellwether Media, Inc. TORQUE and associated logos are trademarks and/or
registered trademarks of Bellwether Media, Inc. SCHOLASTIC, CHILDREN'S PRESS, and associated logos are
trademarks and/or registered trademarks of Scholastic Inc.

Printed in the United States of America, North Mankato, MN.

TABLE OF CONTENTS

TESTING ON THE TRACK

A crowd has gathered at the Nürburgring racetrack in Germany. A driver climbs into a 918 Spyder and puts on his helmet. His crew checks the car and gives it fresh tires. They are set to test the speed of Porsche's new **supercar**.

The timer starts as the driver takes off. He cruises through the forest on the winding track. Steep hills, sharp corners, and changing road conditions test the car's performance. The driver crosses the finish line in under seven minutes. He has set a new lap record!

GO THE DISTANCE
THE NÜRBURGRING'S NORTH LOOP IS
12.9 MILES (20.8 KILOMETERS) LONG.

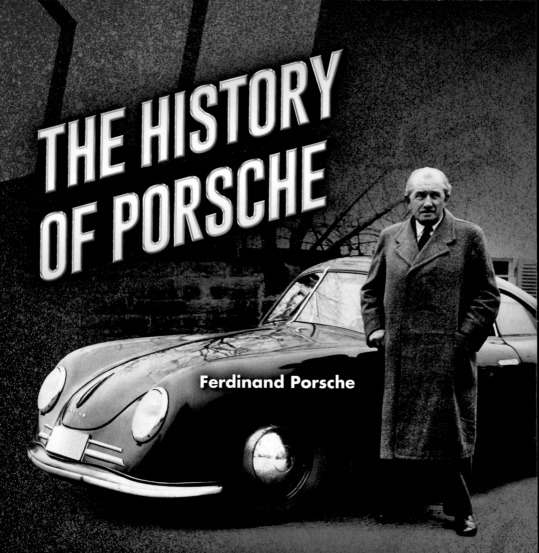

THE HISTORY OF PORSCHE

Ferdinand Porsche

In 1931, Ferdinand Porsche started an **engineering** company in Stuttgart, Germany. Ferdinand and his son, Ferry, first designed cars for other companies. By the late 1940s, the Porsche company started working on its own **models**. Its first sports car rolled out of the factory in 1948. The Porsche 356 became known for its speed and performance.

1948 Porsche 356

DESIGNING A BUG

FERDINAND HELPED DESIGN THE VOLKSWAGEN BEETLE. THIS IS ONE OF THE MOST POPULAR CARS OF ALL TIME.

Volkswagen Beetle

Ferry took over Porsche when Ferdinand passed away in 1951. He continued to design sports cars. Soon, Ferry's son joined the company. He worked on the next Porsche sports car. In 1963, the Porsche 911 was first shown off.

Ferry Porsche and his son

Porsche 911

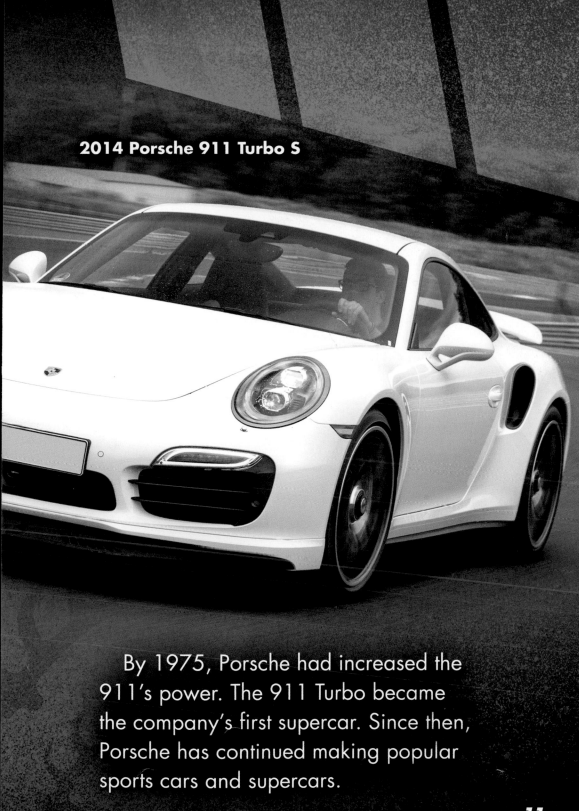

2014 Porsche 911 Turbo S

By 1975, Porsche had increased the 911's power. The 911 Turbo became the company's first supercar. Since then, Porsche has continued making popular sports cars and supercars.

PORSCHE 918 SPYDER

The Porsche 918 Spyder **concept car** was first shown off at the 2010 Geneva Motor Show. It became available to the public three years later. The 918 Spyder combines the power of a race car with the everyday benefits of a **hybrid**. Porsche's new supercar was the first of its kind!

Porsche 918 Spyder concept car

2015 Porsche 918 Spyder

POWERFUL MINDS
THE 918 SPYDER WAS DESIGNED BY THE SAME
TEAM THAT WORKS ON PORSCHE'S RACE CARS.

TECHNOLOGY AND GEAR

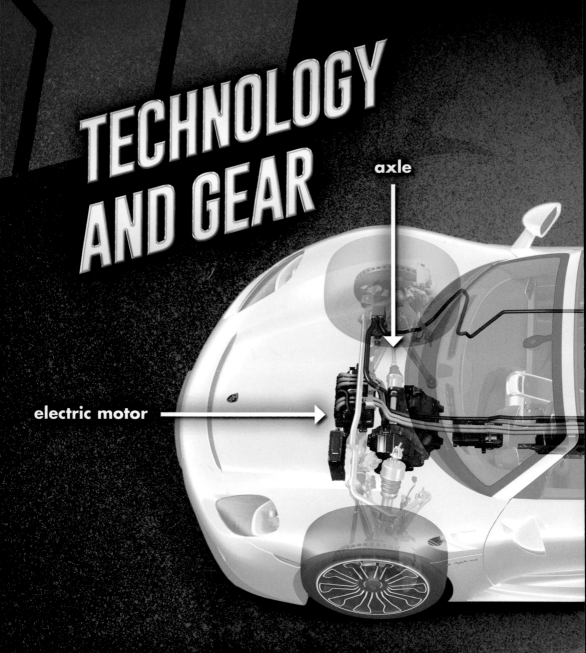

axle

electric motor

The 918 Spyder is made to use as little gas as possible. The car is powered by a **V8 engine** and two **electric motors**. Four settings allow the driver to control how much power comes from the engine and motors.

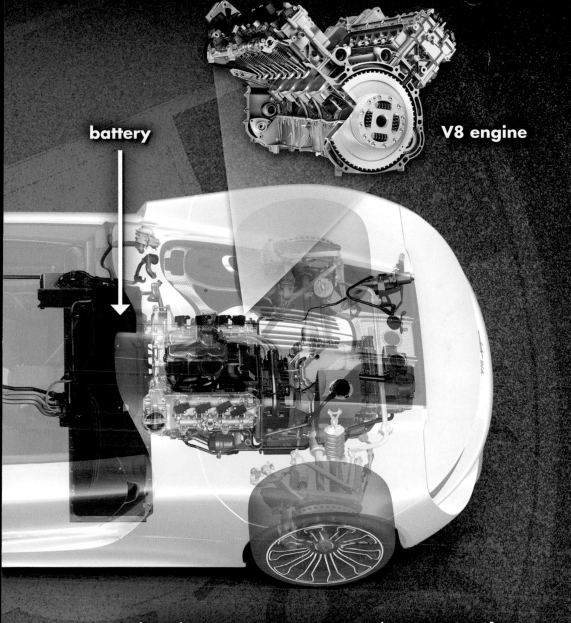

battery

V8 engine

The electric motors are on the car's **axles**.
They are hooked up to a large **battery**.
Alone, the motors can push the 918 Spyder
to 93 miles (150 kilometers) per hour!

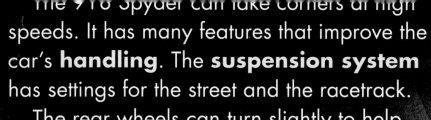

The 918 Spyder can take corners at high speeds. It has many features that improve the car's **handling**. The **suspension system** has settings for the street and the racetrack.

The rear wheels can turn slightly to help the car make tight corners. The rear wheels can also brake to keep the driver in control.

POWERFUL BRAKES
WHEN THE DRIVER BRAKES, THE CAR'S ENERGY HELPS CHARGE THE BATTERY.

The car also has an **aerodynamic** system. Three settings change the positions of the 918 Spyder's **ground effects**. This makes sure the car grips the road in all driving conditions.

A SMART CAR

DRIVERS CAN USE THEIR PHONES TO LOOK UP CAR PERFORMANCE INFORMATION. THEY CAN EVEN MAKE SURE THEIR DOORS ARE LOCKED!

2015 PORSCHE 918 SPYDER SPECIFICATIONS

CAR STYLE	ROADSTER
ENGINE	4.6L V8; TWO ELECTRIC MOTORS
TOP SPEED	214 MILES (344 KILOMETERS) PER HOUR
0 - 60 TIME	ABOUT 2.5 SECONDS
HORSEPOWER	887 HP (661 KILOWATTS) @ 8700 RPM (ENGINE AND MOTORS)
CURB WEIGHT	3,692 POUNDS (1,675 KILOGRAMS)
WIDTH	76.4 INCHES (194 CENTIMETERS)
LENGTH	182.9 INCHES (465 CENTIMETERS)
HEIGHT	46.0 INCHES (117 CENTIMETERS)
WHEEL SIZE	20 INCHES (51 CENTIMETERS) FRONT 21 INCHES (53 CENTIMETERS) BACK
COST	STARTS AT $845,000

TODAY AND THE FUTURE

Fans of the 918 Spyder love the car's power and comfort. Some owners take their car to the racetrack to test the limits of their hybrid supercar. The 918 Spyder's many driving and performance settings give drivers the best experience in all conditions. Though production has ended, this model has led the way for future supercars.

HOW TO SPOT A PORSCHE 918 SPYDER

AIR INTAKES

SPOILER

TOP PIPES

GLOSSARY

aerodynamic—having a shape that can move through air quickly

axles—bars on which wheels turn

battery—a device that supplies machines with electricity

concept car—the first version of a car model

electric motors—machines that use electricity to power a car

engineering—concerned with designing and building cars and other machines

ground effects—panels and flaps on the outside of a car that make it perform and handle better

handling—how a car performs around turns

hybrid—a car with a gas engine and an electric motor; the 918 Spyder has one gas engine and two electric motors.

models—specific kinds of cars

supercar—an expensive and high-performing sports car

suspension system—a series of springs and shocks that help a car grip the road

V8 engine—an engine with 8 cylinders arranged in the shape of a "V"

TO LEARN MORE

AT THE LIBRARY

Harrison, Paul. *Extreme Supercars.* London, U.K.: Arcturus, 2015.

Mulligan, Simon. *Porsche.* New York, N.Y.: PowerKids Press, 2013.

Niver, Heather Moore. *Porsches.* New York, N.Y.: Gareth Stevens Pub., 2012.

ON THE WEB

Learning more about the Porsche 918 Spyder is as easy as 1, 2, 3.

1. Go to www.factsurfer.com.

2. Enter "Porsche 918 Spyder" into the search box.

3. Click the "Surf" button and you will see a list of related web sites.

With factsurfer.com, finding more information is just a click away.

INDEX

The images in this book are reproduced through the courtesy of: Porsche, front cover, pp. 4-5, 6-7, 11, 12-13, 14-15, 16-17, 18-19, 20-21; ullstein bild/ Getty Images, p. 8; VIEW Pictures Ltd/ Alamy, p. 9 (top); f9photos, p. 9 (bottom); dpa picture alliance archive/ Alamy, p. 10 (top); Tupungato, p. 10 (bottom).

HARRIS COUNTY PUBLIC LIBRARY

HARRIS COUNTY PUBLIC LIBRARY
HOUSTON, TEXAS